# MY FIRST
# 500
# WORDS

Wonder House

# alphabet

## Aa

ant

## Bb

ball

## Cc

can

## Dd

drum

## Ee
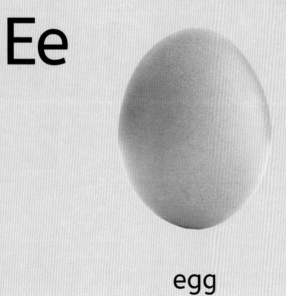
egg

## Ff

flag

# Gg

grapes

# Hh

hat

# Ii

iron

# Jj

jug

# Kk

key

# Ll

leaf

# Mm

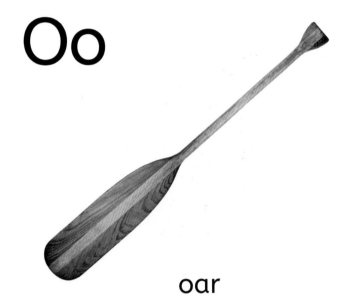

mouse

# Nn

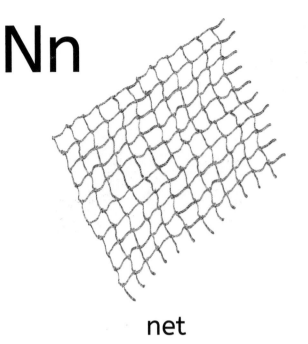

net

# Oo

oar

# Pp

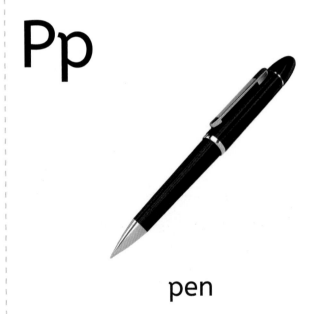

pen

# Qq

quilt

# Rr

rose

# Ss

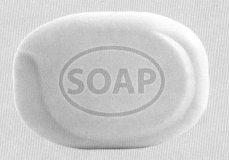

soap

# Tt

tap

# Uu

unicorn

# Vv

violin

# Ww

wheel

# Xx

xylophone

# Yy

yarn

# Zz

zip

# numbers

1 one

2 two

3 three

4 four

5 five

6 six

7 seven

8 eight

9 nine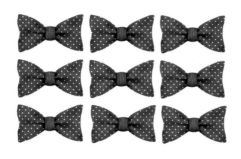

10 ten

# 11
eleven

# 12
twelve

# 13
thirteen

# 14
fourteen

# 15
fifteen

# 16
sixteen

# 17
seventeen

# 18
eighteen

# 19
nineteen

# 20
twenty

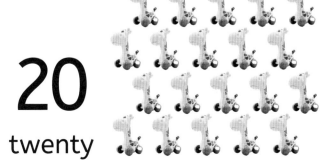

# colors

red

green

pink

orange

yellow

blue

brown

gray

black

violet

white

# shapes

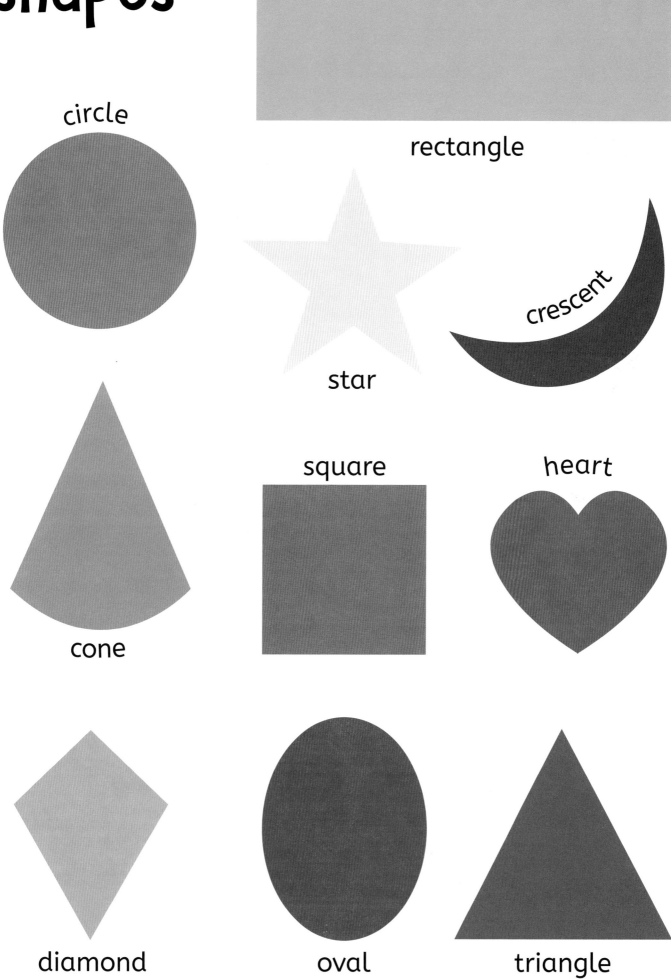

circle

rectangle

star

crescent

cone

square

heart

diamond

oval

triangle

# opposites

hot     cold

inside     outside

slow     fast

heavy     light

soft     hard

dirty     clean

| open | closed |
|------|--------|

| big | small |
|-----|-------|

| happy | sad |
|-------|-----|

| few | many |
|-----|------|

| front | back |
|-------|------|

| empty | full |
|-------|------|

# fruits

apple

mango

grapes

banana

raspberry

orange

cherry

pineapple

watermelon

pomegranate

coconut

grapefruit

peach

guava

avocado

kiwi

strawberry

pear

apricot

papaya

13

# vegetables

cauliflower

broccoli

cabbage

beetroot

eggplant

zucchini

carrot

lettuce

pumpkin

14

onion

celery

french bean

okra

spinach

corn

bell pepper

yam

green pea

radish

potato

15

# food

pizza

chicken

fish

sandwich

macaroni

cornflakes

pie

salad

tofu

ice cream

rice

trail mix

cake

pasta

yogurt

taco

pancake

milk

bread

soup

17

# land transport

bicycle

car

skateboard

crane

bus

motorcycle

dump truck

fire engine

van

truck

ambulance

taxi

train

scooter

# water transport

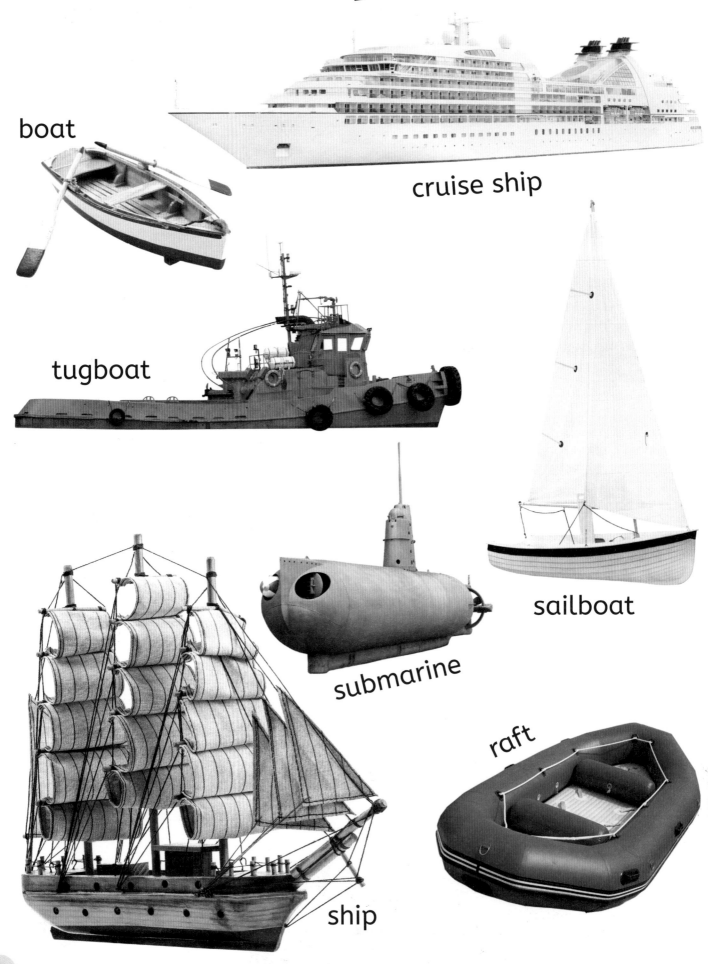

boat

cruise ship

tugboat

sailboat

submarine

raft

ship

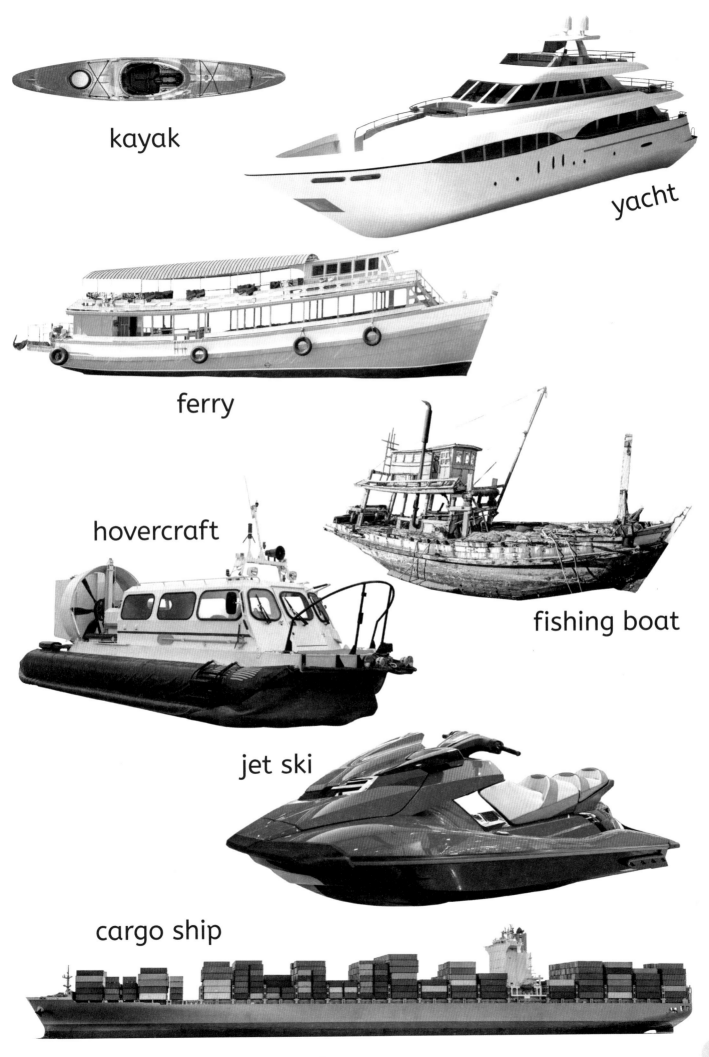

kayak

yacht

ferry

hovercraft

fishing boat

jet ski

cargo ship

# air transport

hot-air balloon

airplane

rocket

helicopter

seaplane

blimp

space
shuttle

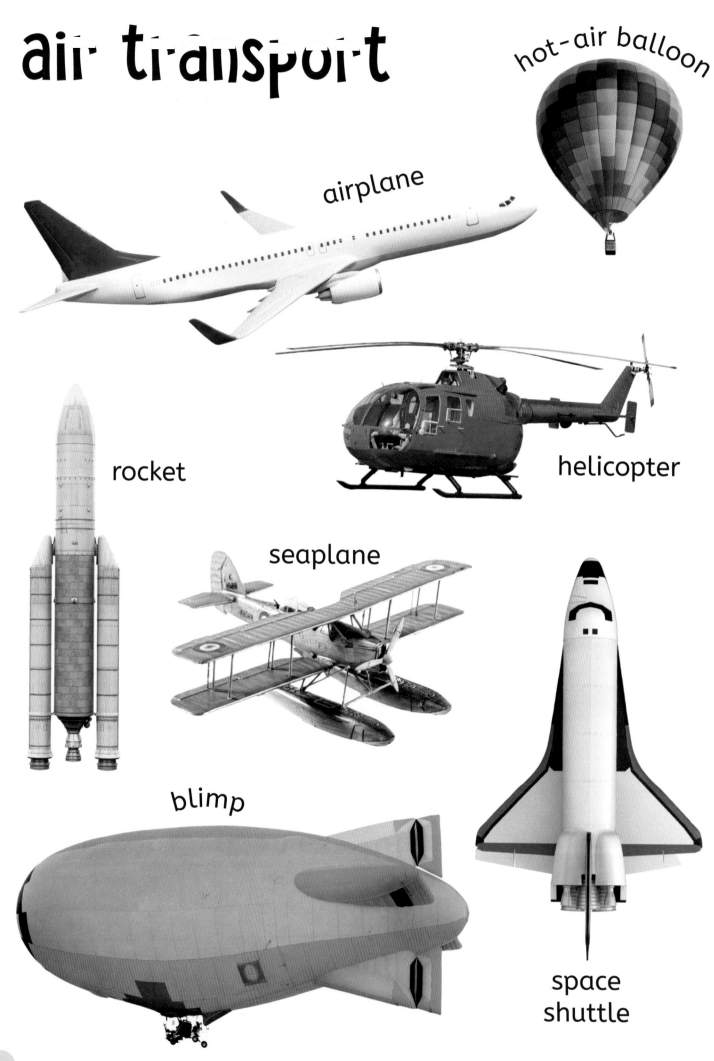

22

# pets

ferret

cat

dog

rabbit

guinea pig

hamster

horse

duck

# farm animals

turkey

cow

goat

llama

camel

hen

buffalo

rooster

bull

goose

donkey

sheep

25

# wild animals

lion

tiger

cheetah

bear

giraffe

koala

gorilla

deer

zebra

rhinoceros

wolf

hippopotamus

kangaroo

fox

panda

elephant

crocodile

27

# sea animals

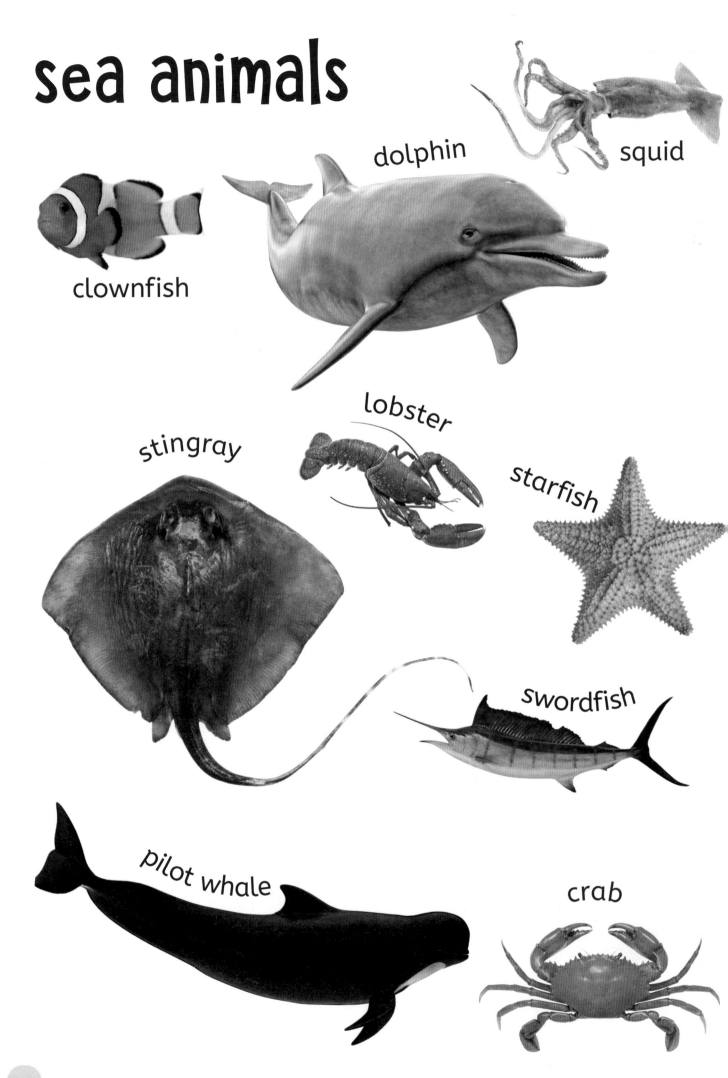

squid

dolphin

clownfish

stingray

lobster

starfish

swordfish

pilot whale

crab

jellyfish

oyster

shark

seal

octopus

seahorse

sea turtle

walrus

eel

# birds

crow

crane

pigeon

hornbill

penguin

sparrow

woodpecker

parrot

peacock

eagle

vulture

ostrich

swan

hummingbird

owl

flamingo

toucan

kingfisher

31

# baby animals

horse foal

lion cub

puppy

parrot chick

cow calf

kit

chick

duckling

deer
fawn

giraffe calf

tiger cub

owlet

kitten

penguin chick

bear cub

lamb

swan cygnet

goat kid

zebra foal

elephant calf

# people at work

farmer

baker

chef

police
officer

teacher

pilot

mechanic

lawyer

photographer

34

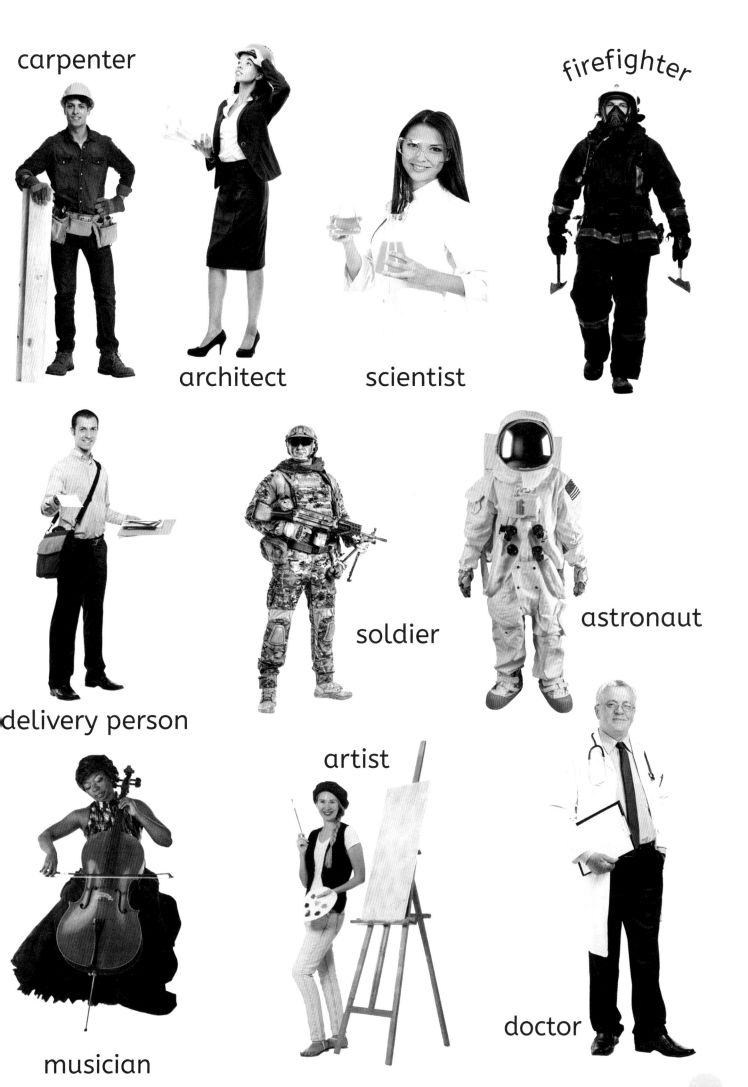

carpenter

architect

scientist

firefighter

delivery person

soldier

astronaut

artist

musician

doctor

35

# toys

kitchen set

blocks

rocking horse

toy train

finger puppets

doll

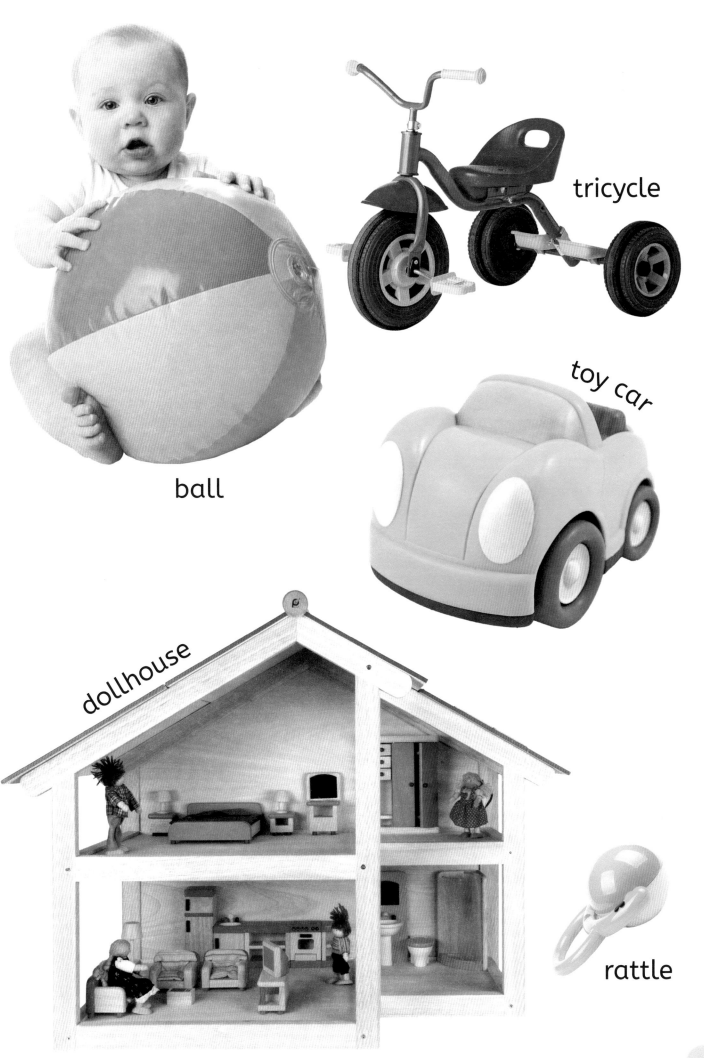

tricycle

toy car

ball

dollhouse

rattle

# baby objects

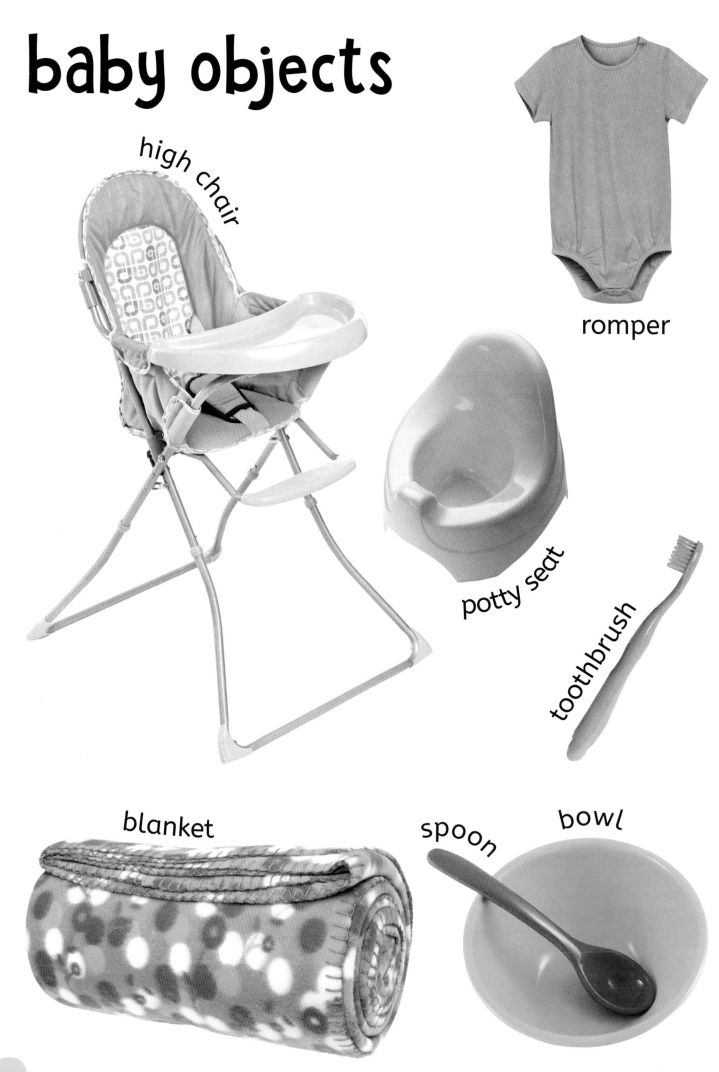

high chair

romper

potty seat

toothbrush

blanket

spoon

bowl

walker

milk bottle

bib

sipper

stroller

baby rocker

# living room

clock

fireplace

carpet

table

television

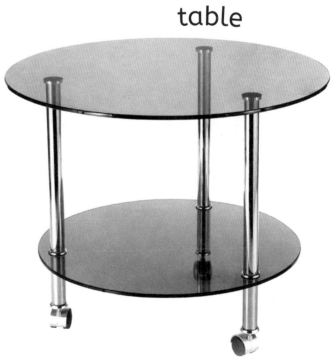

air conditioner

doormat

**WELCOME**

telephone

vase

curtain

sofa

# bedroom

**pillow**

bed

dressing table

table
lamp

## chest of drawers

bedsheet

wardrobe

ironing
board

# bathroom

mirror

bathtub

towel

washbasin

hairbrush

toothpaste

washing machine

shower

shampoo

# kitchen

chimney

sink

apron

frying pan

pressure cooker

dishwasher

toaster

blender

gas stove

kettle

refrigerator

microwave oven

# garden objects

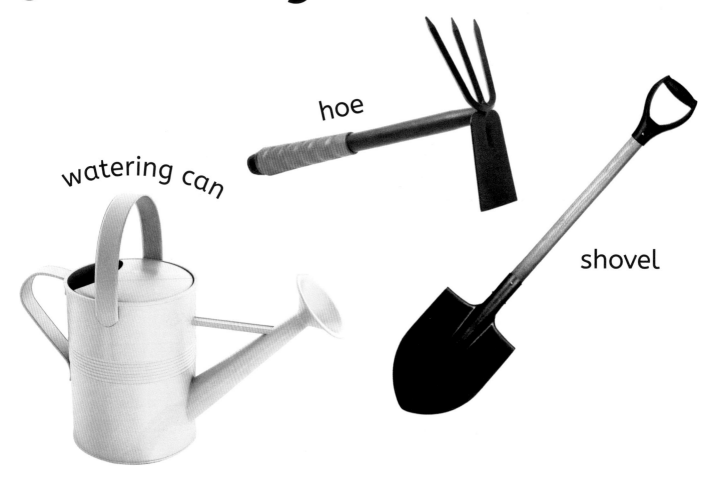

hoe

watering can

shovel

greenhouse

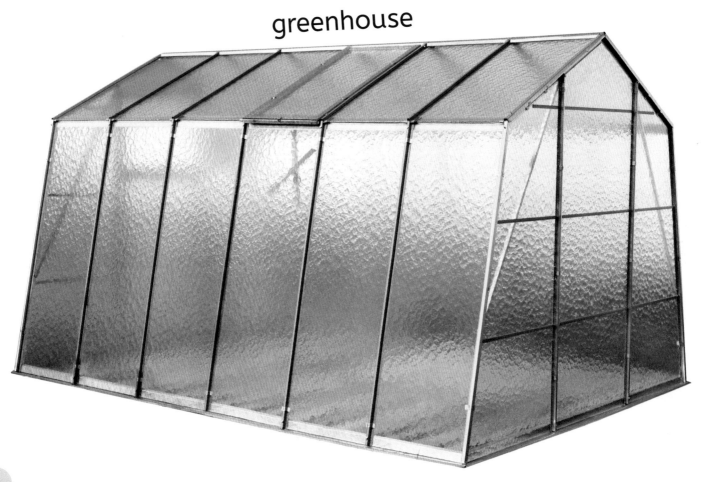

lawn mower

trowel

wheelbarrow

spade

rake

seeds

# school

notebook

blackboard

book

soft board

crayons

chalk

bench

eraser

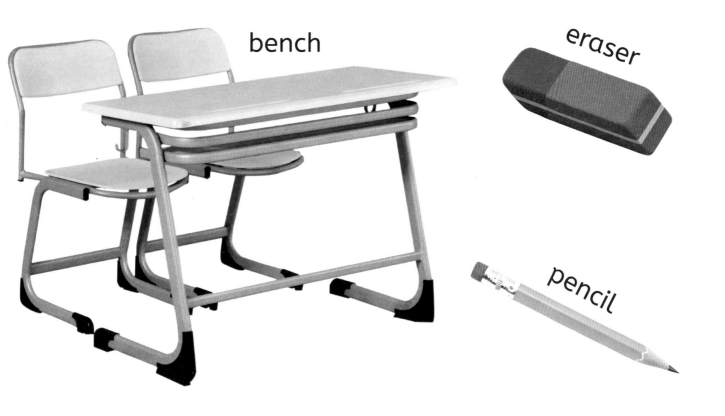

pencil

students

pen

duster

# clothes we wear

t-shirt

scarf

coat

shorts

jeans

dress

trousers

shirt

sweater

skirt

pajamas

# sports

football

basketball

cricket

chess

hockey

table
tennis

cycling

archery

ice skating

gymnastics

karate

golf

rugby

badminton

baseball

# seashore

shell

flippers

diving suit

sun hat

swimming ring

deck chair

umbrella

sandcastle

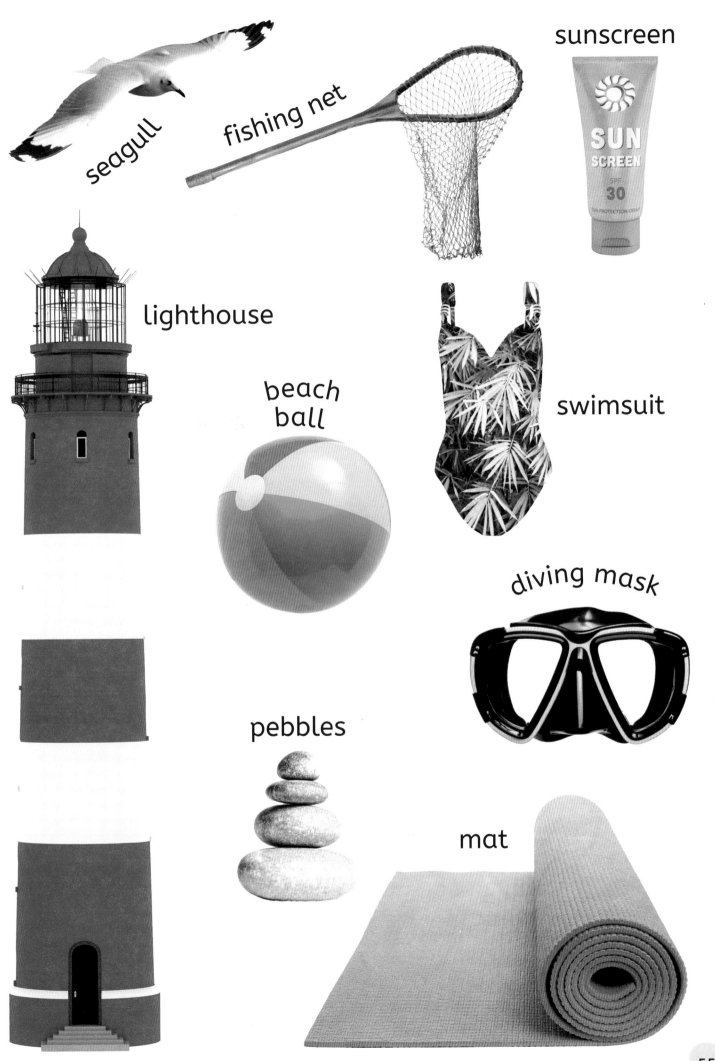

seagull

fishing net

sunscreen

lighthouse

beach ball

swimsuit

diving mask

pebbles

mat

55

# my body

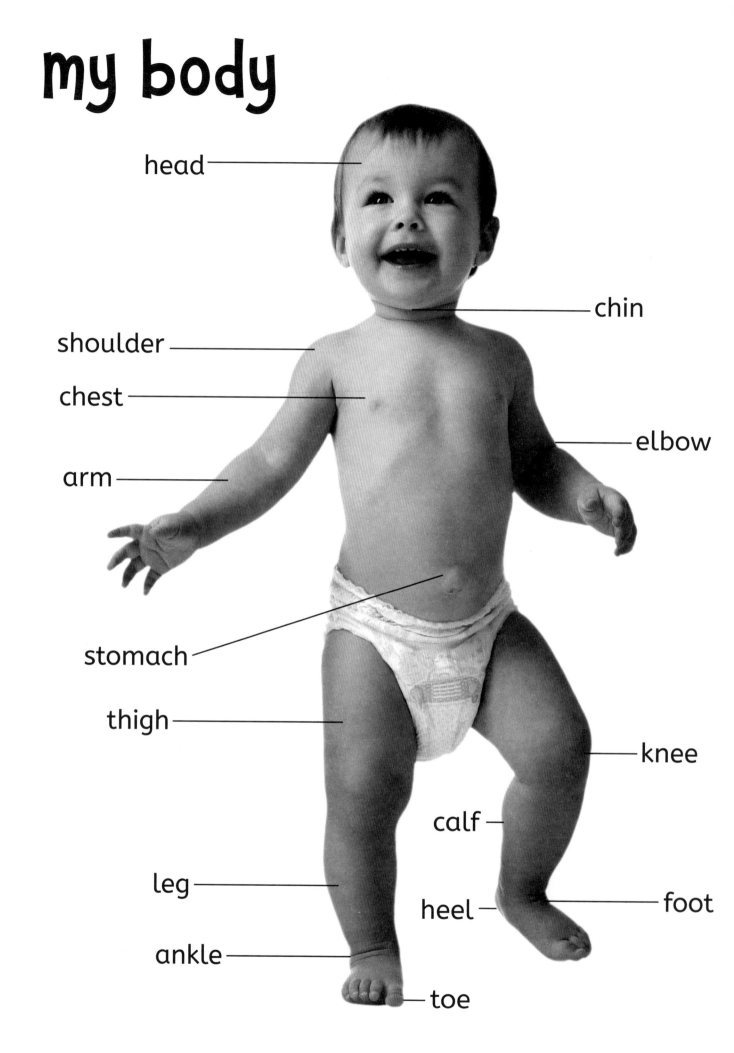

head

chin

shoulder

chest

elbow

arm

stomach

thigh

knee

calf

leg

heel

foot

ankle

toe

# face

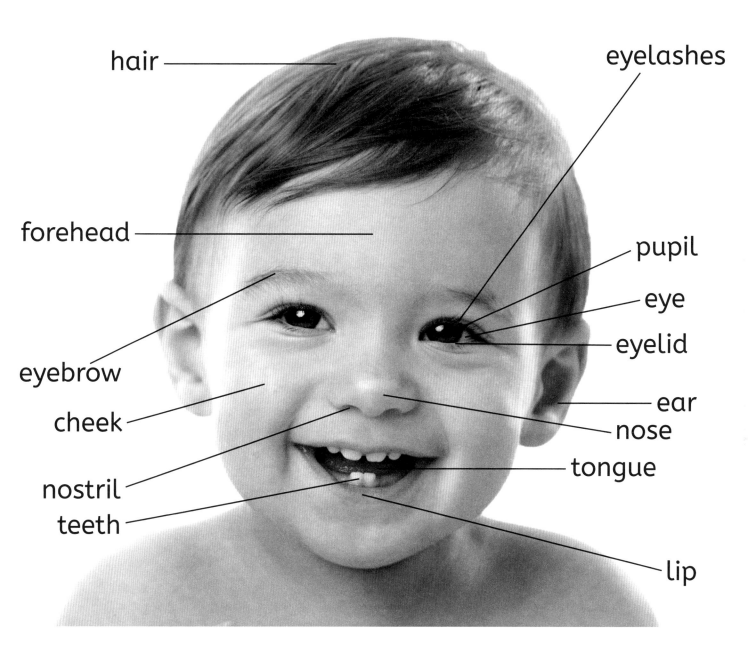

hair

eyelashes

forehead

pupil

eye

eyelid

eyebrow

cheek

ear

nose

nostril

tongue

teeth

lip

# hands

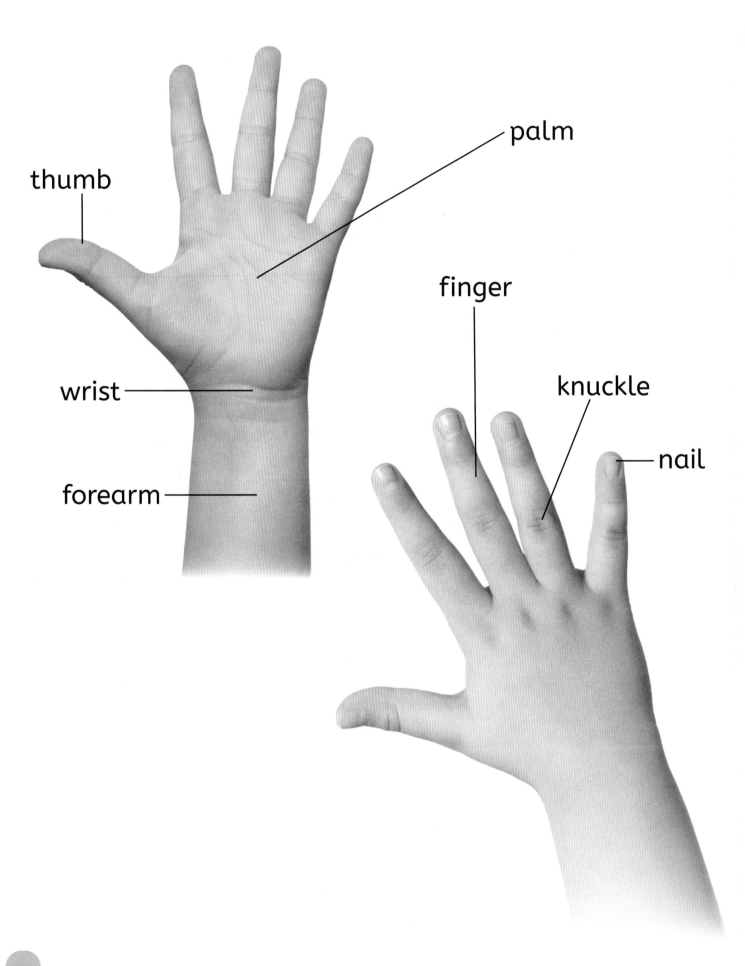

palm

thumb

finger

knuckle

nail

wrist

forearm

# action words

smile

laugh

write

read

eat

drink

talk

frown

cry

walk

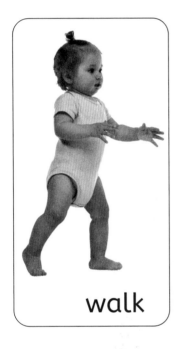

climb

crawl

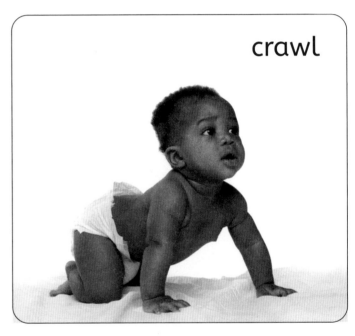

throw

catch

sleep

play

wash

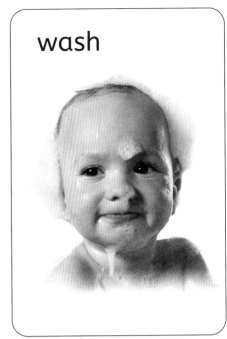

carry

pull

dance

sing

paint

# word list

## a

action words, 59
air transport, 22
air conditioner, 41
airplane, 22
alphabet, 2
ambulance, 19
ankle, 56
ant, 2
apple, 12
apricot, 13
avocado, 13
apron, 44
architect, 35
archery, 52
arm, 56
artist, 35
astronaut, 35

## b

baby animals, 32
baby objects, 38
back, 11
badminton, 53
baker, 34
ball, 2, 37
banana, 12
baseball, 53
basketball, 52
bathroom, 43
bathtub, 43
baby rocker, 39
beach ball, 55
bear, 26
bear cub, 33
bed, 42
bedroom, 42
bedsheet, 42

beetroot, 14
bell pepper, 15
bench, 49
bib, 39
bicycle, 18
big, 11
birds, 30
black, 8
blackboard, 48
blanket, 38
blender, 45
blimp, 22
blocks, 36
blue, 8
boat, 20
book, 48
bowl, 38
bread, 17
broccoli, 14
brown, 8
buffalo, 25
bull, 25
bus, 18

## c

cabbage, 14
cake, 17
camel, 24
can, 2
car, 18
cargo ship, 21
carpenter, 35
carpet, 40
carrot, 14
carry, 61
cat, 23

catch, 60
cauliflower, 14
celery, 15
chalk, 48
cheek, 57
cheetah, 26
chef, 34
cherry, 12
chess, 52
chest, 56
chest of drawers, 42
chick, 32
chicken, 16
chimney, 44
chin, 56
circle, 9
clean, 10
climb, 60
clock, 40
closed, 11
clothes we wear, 50
clownfish, 28
coat, 50
coconut, 13
cold, 10
colors, 8
cone, 9
corn, 15
cornflakes, 16
cow, 24
cow calf, 32
crab, 28
crane, 18
crane, 30
crawl, 60
crayons, 48
crescent, 9
cricket, 52
crocodile, 27
crow, 30
cruise ship, 20
cry, 60

curtain, 41
cycling, 52

## d

dance, 61
deck chair, 54
deer, 26
deer fawn, 32
diamond, 9
delivery person, 35
dirty, 10
dishwasher, 44
diving mask, 55
diving suit, 54
doctor, 35
dog, 23
doll, 36
dollhouse, 37
dolphin, 28
donkey, 25
doormat, 41
dress, 50
dressing table, 42
drink, 59
drum, 2
duck, 23
duckling, 32
dump truck, 19
duster, 49

## e

eagle, 31
ear, 57
eat, 59
eel, 29
egg, 2
eggplant, 14
eight, 6

eighteen, 7
elbow, 56
elephant, 27
elephant calf, 33
eleven, 7
empty, 11
eraser, 49
eye, 57
eyebrow, 57
eyelashes, 57
eyelid, 57

## f

face, 57
farm animals, 24
farmer, 34
fast, 10
ferret, 23
ferry, 21
few, 11
fifteen, 7
finger, 58
finger puppets, 36
fire engine, 19
firefighter, 35
fireplace, 40
fish, 16
fishing boat, 21
fishing net, 55
five, 6
flag, 2
flamingo, 31
flippers, 54
food, 16
foot, 56
football, 52
forearm, 58
four, 6
fourteen, 7
fox, 27